George W. Bush

By Wil Mara

Consultant
Jeanne Clidas, Ph.D.
National Reading Consultant
and
Professor of Reading, SUNY Brockport

Children's Press®
A Division of Scholastic Inc.
New York   Toronto   London   Auckland   Sydney
Mexico City   New Delhi   Hong Kong
Danbury, Connecticut

Designer: Herman Adler Design
Photo Researcher: Caroline Anderson
The photo on the cover shows George W. Bush.

Library of Congress Cataloging-in-Publication Data

Mara, Wil.
  George W. Bush / by Wil Mara.
    p. cm. — (Rookie biographies)
Includes index.
Summary: An introduction to the life of George W. Bush, who became the
forty-third president after the closest presidential race in United States history.
  ISBN 0-516-22852-8 (lib. bdg.)   0-516-27838-X (pbk.)
  1. Bush, George W. (George Walker), 1946—Juvenile literature. 2. Presidents—
United States—Biography—Juvenile literature. 3.
Governors—Texas—Biography—Juvenile literature. [1. Bush, George W.
(George Walker), 1946- 2. Presidents.] I. Title. II. Series: Rookie biography.
  E903 .M365 2003
  973.931—dc21
                                    2002015163

Have you ever thought
about being the president
of the United States?

George W. Bush did. He seemed to be on his way to the presidency (PREZ-uhd-uhnt-see) from the day he was born!

Bush was born on July 6, 1946,
in New Haven, Connecticut.
He was the oldest of six children.

When Bush went to college, he went to Yale University (yoo-nuh-VUR-suh-tee). Many men who became president of the United States went to Yale.

Bush went into the oil business after he finished school.

Oil helps people do many things. It is used to run cars and heat houses.

Bush met Laura Welch while he was in the oil business. She was a teacher and a librarian. They got married in 1977.

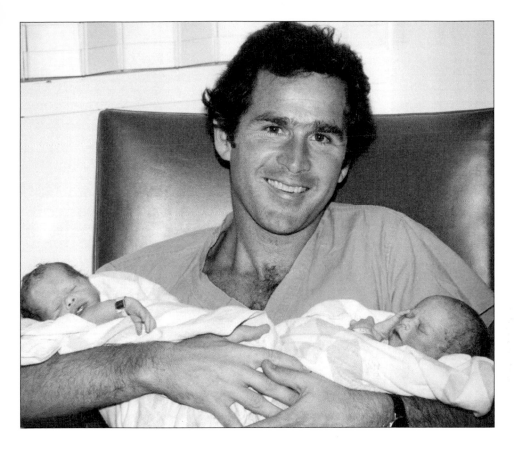

In 1981, they had twin
daughters. Their names
are Barbara and Jenna.

The early 1980s were a strange
time for Bush. He wasn't sure
what he wanted to do with
his life.

He decided to buy a baseball
team in 1988. The team is
called the Texas Rangers.

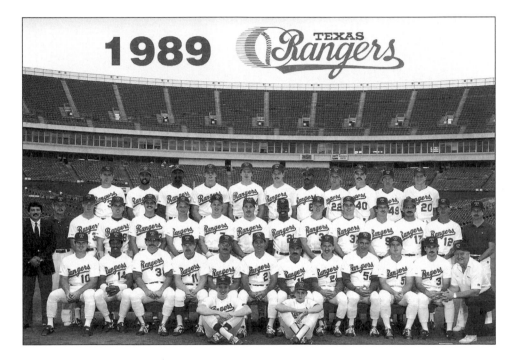

15

Bush went into politics in the early 1990s. People who help to run a community are called politicians (pol-uh-TISH-uhns).

Bush became the governor of Texas in 1994. The governor runs the whole state. It is a very big job!

Bush had never been a politician. Many people thought he would not do a good job, but he did.

When Bush ran for governor again, he won.

In 1999, Bush said he wanted to become president of the United States.

His father, George Herbert
Walker Bush, had been
president, too.

Every president has to have a vice president. The vice president is the second person in charge. Bush chose a man named Dick Cheney to be his vice president.

23

Bush knew it would not be easy becoming president. Another person wanted to be president, too. His name was Al Gore. Gore was a very good politician. Some people thought Gore would win the race.

Americans voted for their new president on November 7, 2000.

The race was the closest in American history. In the end, Bush won.

George W. Bush became
America's 43rd President.
He has become very popular.
He is known for being fair
and for listening to other
people's ideas.

Words You Know

president

George W. Bush

oil

Texas Rangers

politician

governor

vice president

Al Gore

Index

About the Author

More than fifty published books bear Wil Mara's name. He has written both fiction and nonfiction, for both children and adults. He lives with his family in northern New Jersey.

Photo Credits

Photographs © 2003: AP/Wide World Photos: 3, 24, 30 top left, 31 bottom right (J. Scott Applewhite), 6 (Bob Child), 5, 27, 30 top right (Doug Mills), 26 (Toby Talbot); Archive Photos/Getty Images/Rick Wilking/Reuters: 23, 31 bottom left; Baseball Hall of Fame: 15, 30 bottom right; Corbis Images/Wally McNamee: 21; Corbis Sygma/David Woo/Dallas Morning News: 16, 19, 31 top left, 31 top right; Folio, Inc./Phoebe Bell: cover; George Bush Presidential Library: 7, 12; Getty Images: 10, 30 bottom left (Stan Godlewski/Liaison), 13 (Newsmakers), 28 (Mark Wilson); The Image Works/Peter Hvizdak: 9.